MW00826785

Praise Book

8 Innovative Piano Arrangements of Top Contemporary Christian Hits

Mike Springer

Many churches now have "contemporary services" that include Contemporary Christian or Praise music for all or part of the worship. The three volumes of *Not Just Another Praise Book* feature many of the titles used in these services. Lyrics are also included, making these arrangements practical for performance in church.

Not Just Another Praise Book is the fourth addition to the "Not Just Another" series. Beginning with *Not Just Another Scale Book*, three books that hide scales within pieces in all keys, the series continued with *Not Just Another Christmas Book*, three books that feature jazzy arrangements of classic Christmas tunes. The three books of *Not Just Another Jazz Book* include original compositions that feature swing, blues, ragtime, and Latin styles.

Additionally, all of the books are truly unique because they contain innovative and fun orchestrated background tracks for each solo. Included with *Not Just Another Praise Book* is a CD that features MP3 praise band accompaniments. Each piece has three different tracks in the following order.

* For listening, the *Performance Model Track* features the piano and the praise band accompaniment in a complete performance.

* For practicing, the *Practice Tempo Track* features the praise band accompaniment without the piano solo at a slower tempo.

* For performing, the *Performance Tempo Track* features the praise band accompaniment without the piano solo at the performance tempo.

For practice and performance ease, a two-measure drum lead-in is given at the beginning of every track. Metronome markings for both tempos are given at the beginning of each arrangement.

Anyone who has purchased the book has permission to download the files to an MP3 player or burn a CD for personal use. MP3s for the full book are also available for download at **alfred.com/notjustanotherpraise**. The files may not be posted online or distributed over the Internet without written consent from the publisher.

Whether playing the piano part as a solo or with the praise band accompaniments, students will have fun with these pianistic arrangements.

Contents

*for Trietsch Memorial United Methodist Church,
Flower Mound, Texas*

Produced by
Alfred Music
P.O. Box 10003
Van Nuys, CA 91410-0003
alfred.com

Printed in USA.

ISBN-10: 1-4706-1019-1
ISBN-13: 978-1-4706-1019-7

How Great Is Our God

1 Performance Model
2 Practice Tempo (♩ = 66)
3 Performance Tempo (♩ = 80)

Words and Music by Jesse Reeves,
Chris Tomlin and Ed Cash
Arr. Mike Springer

With passion

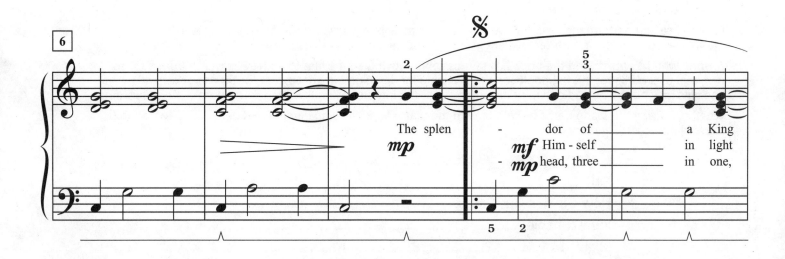

The splen - dor of_____ a King
Him - self_____ in light
head, three_____ in one,

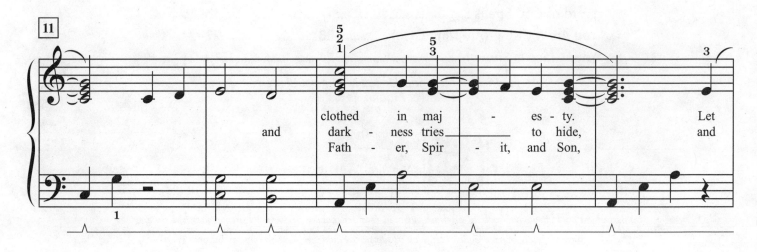

and clothed in maj - es - ty.
and dark - ness tries_____ to hide, Let
Fath - er, Spir - it, and Son, and

16

all the earth re - joice,
trem-bles at His voice
Li - on and the Lamb,

all the earth re-joice.
trem-bles at His voice.
Li - on and the Lamb.

1. He wraps

21 **2., 3.**

How great is our God! Sing with me: How

26

great is our God! And all will see how great, how great

32 *to Coda* ⊕ *D.S. al Coda*

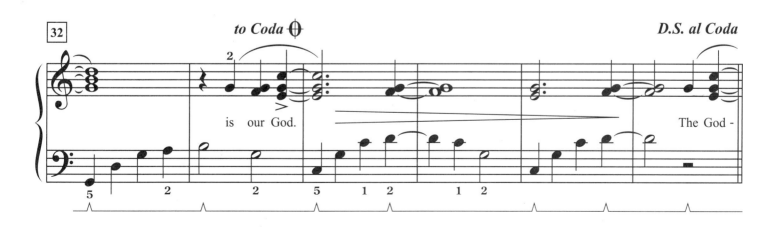

is our God. The God -

Coda

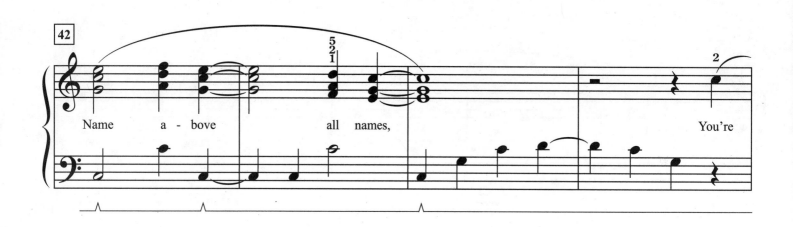

Name a - bove all names,   You're

wor - thy of all praise.   My heart will sing:

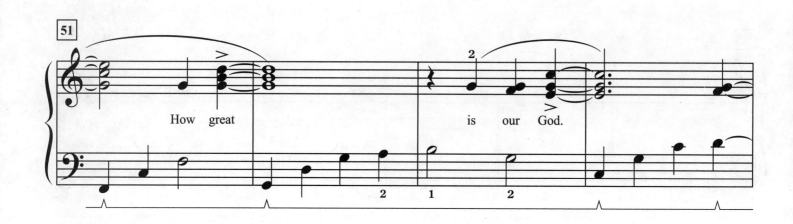

How great   is our God.

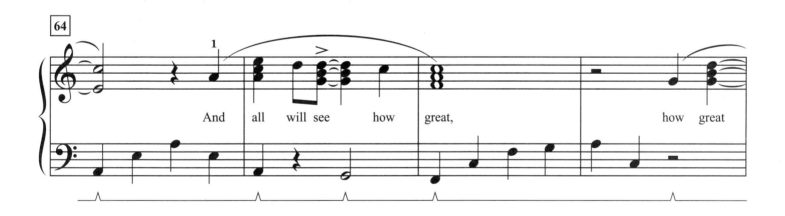
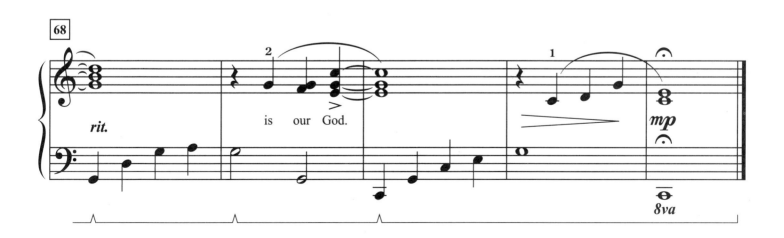

Indescribable

4 Performance Model
5 Practice Tempo (♩ = 132)
6 Performance Tempo (♩ = 176)

Words and Music by
Jesse Reeves and Laura Story
Arr. Mike Springer

8

Mighty to Save

7 Performance Model
8 Practice Tempo (♩ = 60)
9 Performance Tempo (♩ = 80)

Words and Music by
Reuben Morgan and Ben Fielding
Arr. Mike Springer

for the glor - y 58 of the ris - en King. 59 60

Sav - ior, He can move the moun - tains. My God is

mf 62 63 64

migh - ty to save, 66 He is migh - ty to save! 68

67

Migh - ty to save, 70 He is migh - ty to save! 72 73

rit. 71 *mp*

Open the Eyes of My Heart

10 Performance Model
11 Practice Tempo (♩ = 88)
12 Performance Tempo (♩ = 104)

Words and Music by Paul Baloche
Arr. Mike Springer

With passion

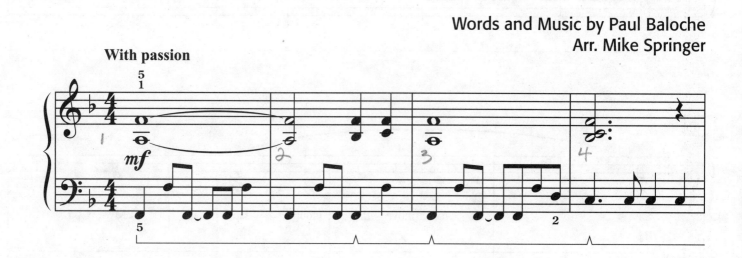

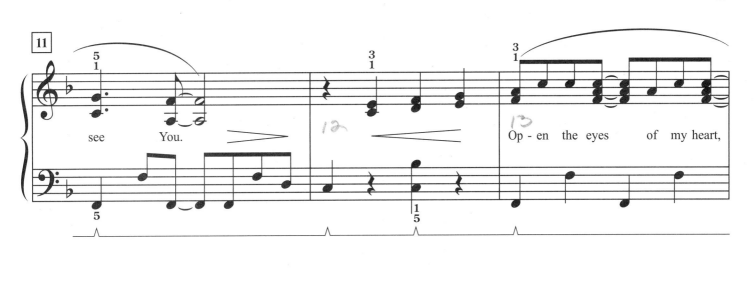

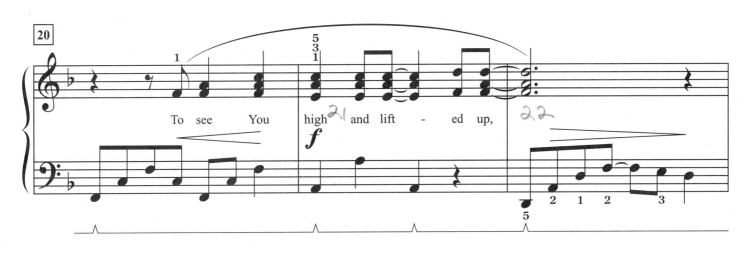

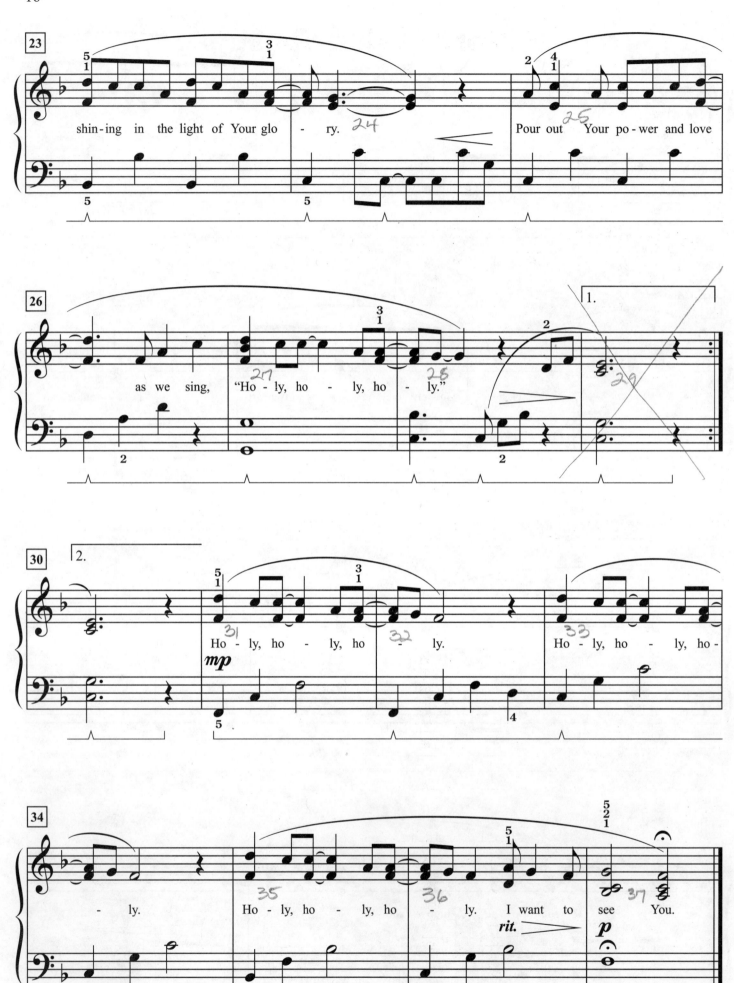

Word of God Speak

13 Performance Model
14 Practice Tempo (♩ = 60)
15 Performance Tempo (♩ = 72)

Words and Music by
Peter Kipley and Bart Millard
Arr. Mike Springer

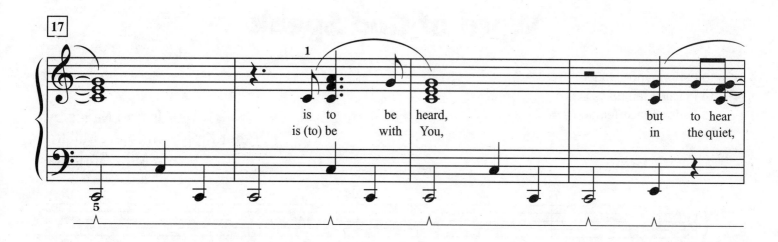

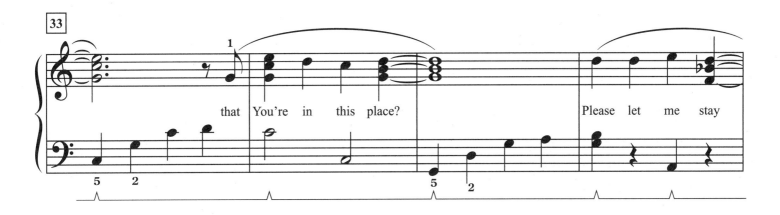

that You're in this place? Please let me stay

and rest in Your ho - li - ness. Word of God, speak.

dim. I'm find - ing my - self at a loss for

words, and the fun - ny thing is, it's o - kay.

Shout to the Lord

16 Performance Model
17 Practice Tempo (♩ = 66)
18 Performance Tempo (♩ = 80)

Words and Music by Darlene Zschech
Arr. Mike Springer

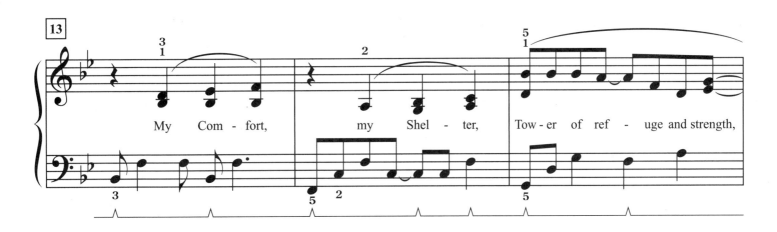

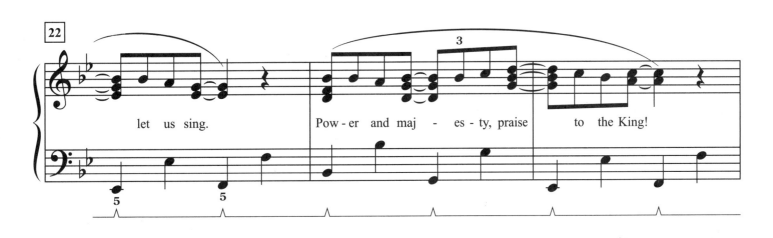

Moun-tains bow down and the seas will roar at the sound_____ of Your

name_____ I sing for joy at the work of Your hands. For -

ev - er I'll love You, for - ev - er I'll stand. Noth-ing com-pares to the prom-

- ise I have in You!

I sing for joy at the work of Your hands, for-ev-er I'll love You, for-ev-

-er I'll stand. Noth-ing com-pares to the prom - ise I have.

Noth-ing com-pares to the prom - ise I have. Noth-ing com-pares to the prom-

-ise I have in You.

Your Grace Is Enough

19 Performance Model
20 Practice Tempo (♩ = 116)
21 Performance Tempo (♩ = 138)

Words and Music by Matt Maher
Arr. Mike Springer

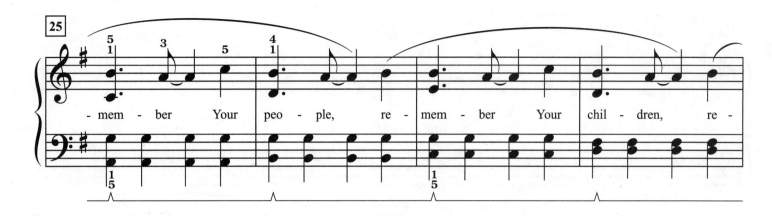

-mem - ber Your peo - ple, re - mem - ber Your chil - dren, re -

mem - ber Your prom - ise, oh God. Your

grace is e - nough, Your grace is e - nough, Your

grace is e - nough for ___ me.

You Are My King
(Amazing Love)

22 Performance Model
23 Practice Tempo (♩ = 120)
24 Performance Tempo (♩ = 144)

Words and Music by
Billy James Foote
Arr. Mike Springer

Joyfully!

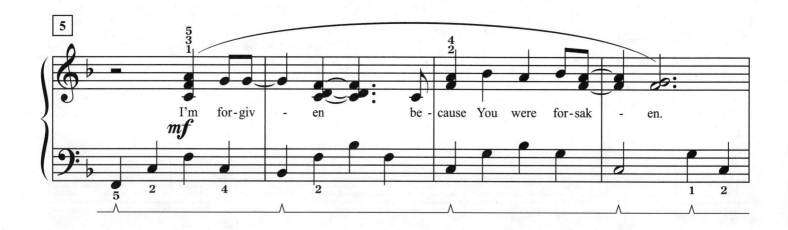

I'm for-giv - en be - cause You were for-sak - en.

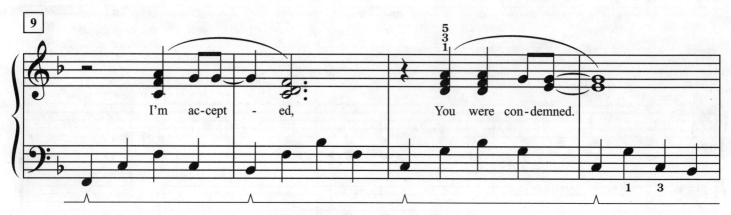

I'm ac-cept - ed, You were con-demned.

I'm a-live and well, Your spir-it is with-in me be-

cause You died and rose a-gain.

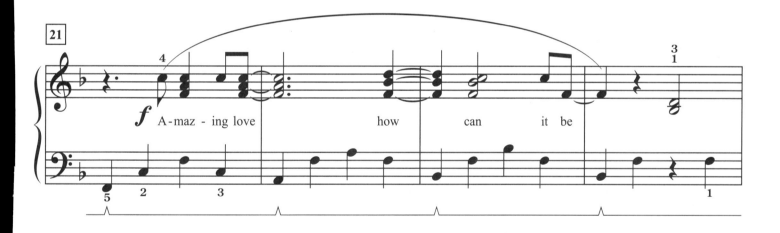

A-maz-ing love how can it be

that You, my King, would die for me?

A - maz - ing love, I know it's true.

It's my joy to hon - or You, in all I

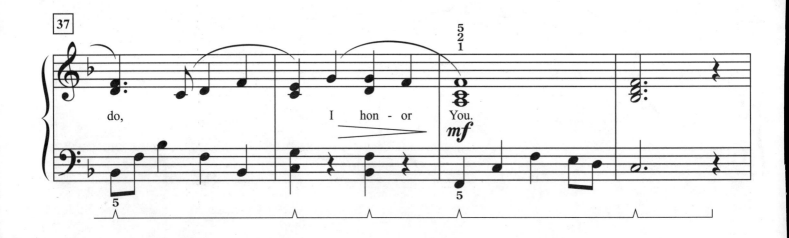

do, I hon - or You.
mf

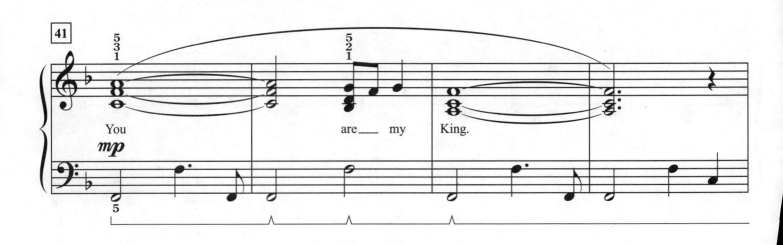

You are___ my King.
mp

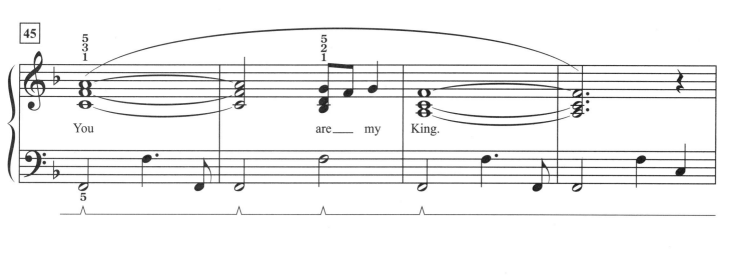

You ... are__ my King.

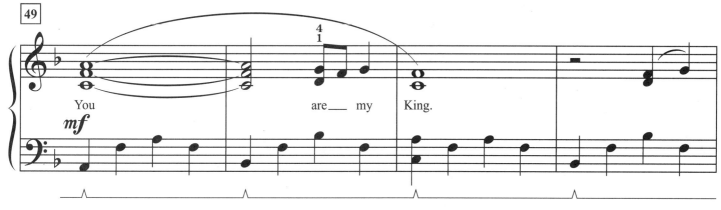

You ... are__ my King.

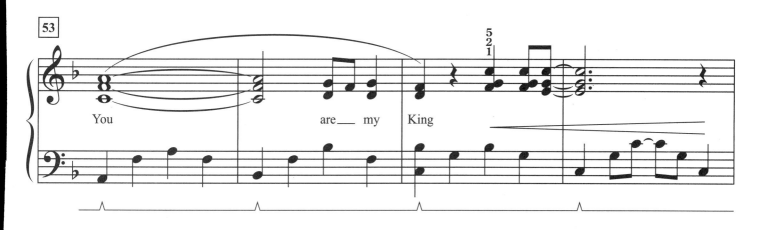

You ... are__ my King

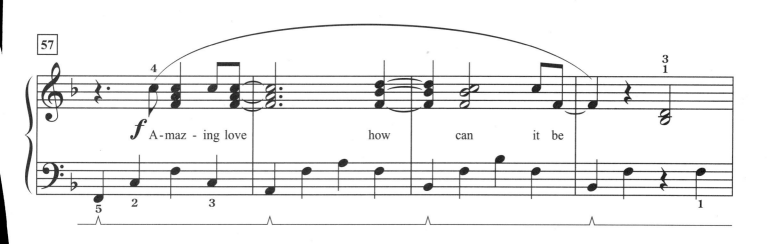

A-maz - ing love ... how ... can ... it ... be

that You my King, would die for me?

A-maz-ing love, I know it's true.

It's my joy to hon - or You, in all I

do, I hon - or You.

rit. *mf* *mp*